Cat and Dog on Playground Patrol

"Take turns. Play fair."

2

"Let's talk things over!"

3

"Wait! That is not safe.
I will get the ball."

"Here is a ball you *can* kick."

"Be safe! Watch where you are going."

"Sit down. Go feet first down the slide."

"Recess is fun when we follow the rules!"